Sharks

Contents **Page**

Sharks	2-3
Prey	4-5
Catching sharks	6-7
Shark parts	8-9
Breeding	10-11
Rays	12-13
Pollution	14
Diving with sharks	15
Saving sharks	16

written by John Lockyer

Red Rocket Readers™
Engineered by Flying Start Books

Sharks can be big and they can be small. Sharks swim in the sea. If a shark stops still, it will sink.

There are lots of fish in the sea, but sharks are not like them. Sharks do not have bones.

Some sharks have many teeth, but they drop out a lot. A new tooth can grow in one day.

prey

Sharks catch food to eat. They like to eat fish. They will eat crabs, squid, and birds, too.

Some people catch sharks with hooks and big nets. They catch sharks to eat. They make pet food with sharks, too.

catching sharks

Shark fins can be cut off to make shark fin broth. Shark skin is made into bags and shoes.

Humans will not go into the sea if a shark is there. They want to kill the shark so they can swim.

The sea is the shark's home. So, it is good to check out the spot when you want to swim.

We catch and kill too many sharks. Now, sharks are at risk. When sharks are four years old, they can have pups.

Many sharks get stuck on hooks or in nets when they have not had pups yet. Sharks will not have pups in water that is not clean.

Sharks like to eat rays and rays like to eat clams. With less sharks, there are more rays - and with more rays, there are less clams.

rays

Some humans put poles in the water so the rays cannot eat all the clams.

pollution

Plastic waste can kill sharks. Sharks eat the plastic waste or eat fish that have fed on it.

You can swim with sharks, but you should be inside a steel box so the shark can not get to you.

saving sharks

Can we save sharks? We can save sharks if we do not buy stuff that is made out of them.